China Suite
and other Poems

Gillian Bickley

Proverse Hong Kong

China Suite and other Poems is Gillian Bickley's fourth collection of poems in which she responds to people, art and life, creating a record of her particular space in time. Hong Kong, Beijing, Shanghai, Sukhothai, Honolulu, Mexico City, northernmost Scotland, Andorra are among the places. Intimates and strangers are the people. She is interested as much in a mother and son seen for some seconds on a bridge in Shanghai as in the emotions flowing between performer and conductor throughout a concert, and the interpretation one creative artist gives to that of another's work. She values the records we all make:—the heritage we may or may not preserve, what we choose to reveal of our lives, the constant interpretative understanding of the personal as well as the historical past, and the sacredness of memory. Here we find observation and reflection—on current affairs as well as people and places—and also the frisson produced by five "skulls" in a window, a funeral owl caught in hire-car headlights, and the realization that classical stories are re-enacted in our own lives.

Supported by

The Hong Kong Arts Development Council fully supports freedom of artistic expression. The views and opinions expressed in this project do not represent the stand of the Council.

China Suite
and other Poems

Gillian Bickley

Proverse Hong Kong

China Suite and Other Poems
by Gillian Bickley
2nd pbk ed published in Hong Kong by Proverse Hong Kong,
December 2016.

ISBN-13: 978-988-8228-55-3
Available from https://www.createspace.com/6650716

1st published in pbk (w. 2 audio CDs of the author reading all poems in the collection) in Hong Kong by Proverse Hong Kong, 25 November 2009
Web site: www.proversepublishing.com

ISBN-13: 978-988-17724-9-7

Enquiries: Proverse Hong Kong, P.O. Box 259, Tung Chung Post Office, Tung Chung, Lantau, NT, Hong Kong SAR. E-mail: proverse@netvigator.com
Web site: www.proversepublishing.com

Page design by Proverse Hong Kong.
Cover and CD labels design by Errol Patrick Hugh.
Cover photograph by and © Proverse Hong Kong.

Proverse Hong Kong

British Library Cataloguing in Publication Data (for 1st edition)

Bickley, Gillian
China suite and other poems.
1. Interpersonal relations--Poetry. 2. Hong Kong (China)--
Poetry. 3. China--Poetry.
I. Title
821.9'14-dc22

ISBN-13: 9789881772497

Recommendation

"China Suite and other Poems" by Gillian Bickley offers a unique, poetic perspective on Hong Kong and China. Part observations on people, part commentary, divining the divine, and the not-so-divine, the poetry in this collection will help us to round out our own view of this part of the world...

That much I can say, but I want to say more. I thought that, to recommend a book of poetry, I needed to know (being a writer of prose myself, primarily) what poetry is.
And so, to Google.

So What is poetry?
Samuel Johnson says Poetry is the art of uniting pleasure with truth.
Leonard Cohen says Poetry is just the evidence of life.
Plato says Poetry is nearer to vital truth than history.

These are lofty sentiments, but I refuse to be intimidated!

John Keats says Poetry should be great and unobtrusive,
a thing which enters into one's soul,
and does not startle it or amaze it with itself,
but with its subject.

And What can poetry do?
T. S. Eliot says Genuine poetry can communicate before it is understood.
Keats [again] says Poetry should strike the reader as a wording of his own highest thoughts, and appear almost a remembrance.

5

So I will end this recommendation by offering up an ancient Buddhist poem (in rhyme, no less):

Not every poem's good because it's ancient,
Nor mayst thou blame it just because it's new,
Fair critics test, and prove, and so pass judgment;
Fools praise or blame as they hear others do.

And this, from Kahlil Gibran:

A poet is a bird of unearthly excellence, who escapes from his celestial realm and arrives in this world warbling. If we do not cherish him, he spreads his wings and flies back to his homeland.

I am not an expert in poetry. If anyone claimed to be one, I would look at them sideways.
But I say Gillian Bickley is a poet.
And you are lucky to have this poetry in your hand.

Karmel Schreyer
Hong Kong
September 2009
HKADC Examiner (Literary Arts)

Karmel Schreyer has written over thirty books, children's, young-adult fiction, information/novelty and history/memoir ('By the Banks of the Brokenhead'). She contributes to magazines and newspapers and writes educational materials for markets in Canada and Asia.

China Suite and other Poems by Gillian Bickley. Table of Contents

Recommendation by Karmel Schreyer		5
Preface by Elbert S. P. Lee		11
	CHINA SUITE	page
	Author's Acknowledgements	15
1.	Wish you were here in Hong Kong!	19
2.	Mythical Creatures	22
3.	Passing beauty (salon-wards): Caged Jaguar and free spotted girl	23
4.	Ambiguous Communication: Crossing the road to the Library	24
5.	David at Tai Po Market KCR Station	25
6.	Tai Po Lady	27
7.	Seen in Shanghai	28
8.	Public Secrets at the Post Office	33
9.	A Relative Quiet at Yam O	34
10.	Wisdom at a Concert Meeting a Meet Applause *or* Concerted Wisdom	35
11.	Ferris wheel at night	38
12.	Street Triptych	39
13.	Gangways	40
14.	The Smell of Germolene	41
15.	Microphone	43
16.	Familiarity	44
17.	Cornwall Road Garden	45
18.	Morrison 200th Anniversary Conference	47
19.	Shooting Star *or* Heritage Hindered	49
20.	Fisherwoman: One Ashes to Water	53

21.	Fisherwoman: Two She loved the Sea	53
22.	Communicable Smile	56
23.	On the bus to Tuen Mun	57
24.	Five skulls at the window	58
25.	Security unmanned	59
26.	Applause: *or* A simply ambiguous life	60
27.	Truth rules?	62
28.	Waving Goodbye	63
29.	The flute-player: sweet and low	64
30.	Sipping Tea at the Tea Museum, Hong Kong Park	66
31.	"You can be like God"	66
32.	Weathervane	67
33.	Double-take: recycled reading	68
34.	Beggarly Smile	70
35.	Patterns in a Garden Suburb	71
36.	Torch the Nest Egg!	72
37.	Beijing in Blossom Time	74
38.	Breakfast time at the Friendship Hotel	76
	OTHER POEMS	
39.	Rose-petals: Dali and Carroll	79
40.	Tengmalm's (Funeral) Owl	81
41.	Knowing her Name	85
42.	Penates	86
43.	Word-diggers	88
44.	Caring Professionals	91
45.	Terrorism and thought control	93
46.	Blogs (Web logs)	94
47.	Anthropological Museum	96
48.	Image[ination]	97
49.	Imaginary Existence	98
50.	The Hukilau	99
51.	Pollarded: Frank Coluccio Construction	100

8

52.	Stop Requested	101
53.	Spirit and Sense	102
54.	Cassandra	103
55.	Understanding Her	104
56.	Leaving Clothes	105
57.	Concerns	106
58.	Cat-calls	107
59.	Sukhothai	108
60.	Pumpkin man	109

Notes	111
About the Author	117
About the Publishers and the Proverse Literary Prizes	119

9

Preface

The title of Gillian Bickley's fourth volume of poems, *China Suite and other Poems*, will not turn heads. But titles, like names and appearances, can be misleading. *China Suite and other Poems* is best described as a plain-looking treasure-box. But it is what is in it that counts—a collection of poems that are precious and rare. This collection of poems is nothing less than the carefully focused intersections of geography, the human intellect, and the human heart –those of the author herself and of the individuals she came across on her path of traveling. It is not hard to tell, these poems are the result of long years of traveling—or better, of really living, seeing, and feeling things and places that are apparently commonplace, but are deeply saturated with meaning and human affect.

Like gemstones freshly dug out of a quarry, the poems in this volume are unpretentious, direct, and may even be described as raw. As such, the forms they assume are multifaceted not unlike life itself. The use of language is simple and the choice of material is familiar. The poems are about mundane events, things, and people that can easily go by without being noticed. But it is precisely this ability to hide awe behind this commonness that makes the reading of her poems often a deeply touching and soul-searching experience. A case in point can be found in 'Mythical creatures', Gillian juxtaposes the common meanings of monsters, ghouls, angels, parents, and children to ask what we really don't know about these creatures—what may appear common is really mythical.

At hand is a collection of poems that may be likened to carefully hand picked and rare gems preserved in their natural states. The poems here remind me of the later works of Picasso which are often seen as simple, daring, unpretentious,

11

experimental, and therefore, childlike—some kind of return to the most creative and original. In 'Passing beauty (salon-wards): Caged jaguar and the free spotted girl', playfully, Gillian raises existential questions about beauty as she made allusion to her (our) desire to capture, by "taking pictures", the beauty of the caged spotted photogenic jaguar and her (our) own concern for beauty via the "salon"—both beauties are equally elusive of capture—done instantaneously but short-lived, and for the individuals involved, perhaps also necessarily "unfree"?

In reading her poems, awaiting you between the pages is always a new dawn in one's reading experience in the form of a surprise, a shock, a wakeup call, and at times, a gentle touch. Whatever they may be, one can be certain that they are calculated to release charges at the various depths of the human psyche. It is these qualities of her poems that compel the reader to move from poem to poem without pause, in her book.

There is also another quality in Gillian's poems that is worth commending. Some of the gemstones in her treasure box are diamonds incompletely cut in deliberation to allow for reader participation. These poems are set up beautifully to capture our attention but are fluid and open enough to let you make what you want to make out of them. 'Ambiguous communication: Crossing the road to the library' and 'Tai Po lady' are cases in point. In these poems, the author is no longer more knowledgeable than the reader about what she writes. In this special way, Gillian shares with us her bewilderment of day-to-day encounters at crossroads in life and the mystery involved in what one thinks one knows about the other. For Gillian, these encounters may be brief but they are never deprived of human significance.

Most impressive about Gillian's poems is the

ease with which she glides across the different genres of human experiences—from the most repugnant, to the most charming, from the most hidden, to the most apparent. This is the crown jewel, if you like, of this collection. In her work, the psychological boundaries that separate culture from culture, clan from clan, and individual from individual are completely set aside. An unnoticed observer, she trespasses ethnic taboos and social no-nos, and writes down whatever she sees without getting caught—in a graceful way. This is most evident in the first poem of this collection, 'Wish you were here in Hong Kong', where she has completely transcended the rigid rules of poetry, of social boundaries, and of ethnic preoccupations. In a poem from a previous volume of Gillian's, the poet imagines herself speaking as Tin Hau, the queen of heaven of the southern seas, and with compassionate eyes, she watches how men fail. That Tin Hau is loving, but somewhat distant—her world is speakable but untouchable. But in this collection, some important changes have taken place. Perhaps it can be described like this: this time, in Gillian's own eyes, everything under the sun—from a cozy casual day-to-day encounter, to a family with a Down's syndrome child, from the simple action of writing a letter at the post office, to a man lasciviously consuming a cigarette in the street, they are the speakable and touchable treasures of Tin Hau's unspeakable heaven.

Elbert Siu Ping Lee, Ph.D.
1 October 2009
National Day, The 60th Anniversary of The People's Republic of China

Elbert Siu Ping Lee teaches psychology at the Hong Kong Campus of Upper Iowa University and is a member of the adjunct faculty. His poetry collection, *Rain on the Pacific*

Coast, was published by Proverse in 2013 and received publication support from Hong Kong Arts Development Council. He occasionally contributes poems and feature articles to magazines. Some of his work can be found in *Asian Cha* and *Macao Poetry* (both online English literary and poetry magazines). His poems appear in *Hong Kong Poems, an English-German anthology* (Stauffenburgs, 2007) and in *Fifty/Fifty: A new anthology of Hong Kong writing* (Haven Books, 2008).

14

Author's Acknowledgements

Having had parents, aunts and great-aunts who supported my interest in words since I was very young, I have always loved reading poetry and I first shared my own with them. The moral as well as financial support of the Hong Kong Arts Development Council has much more recently been extremely encouraging as have the friendship and energy of the voluntary organizers of the Hong Kong poetry group, Outloud and the interest of those who come to read and listen at their monthly sessions held at the Hong Kong Festival Fringe Club.

I am grateful for the interesting and thoughtful contributions to this book by neighbour and fellow-writer Karmel Schreyer and fellow poet and academic Elbert S. P. Lee, who recently organised a successful and charming first Peng Chau Carnival full of dance, poetry, song and other delights on a neighbouring island. I am grateful to Canadian Hong Kong architect Errol Patrick Hugh for the cover design and to the Chinese University of Hong Kong Press for again distributing my work.

I cannot give enough thanks to Verner Bickley, my husband, for his constant companionship, advice and love.

15

16

2006

17

18

Wish you were here in Hong Kong![1]

I shall always be disappointed
that my parents came once only to Hong Kong;
rejecting, as it seemed,
all the things I had to share with them, here:

Densely packed mimosa along Siu Wo Road;

The happy wanderer, like Johnny Apple-seed,
with bundle on stick, bouncing down the road
to his public housing estate space
at the end of the day;

Cats he fed tenderly from the back of his truck,
parked at a green garden near a scenic lookout,
and our concern when they disappeared;

Dog excreta in the grass;

The public lavatory with no drainage system,
built by mistake, then reduced to its original intention,
a place for literate dogs to leave their packages;

Noisy buffalo chomping on young trees;

Homing pigeons taking time off, at the side of the path;

Views of the Buddhist Christian study centre, across a
deep valley;

And in the distance, the entrancing expanse of an
encircling mountain range;

The gleaming false gold of a butterfly chrysalis;

19

Make-shift illegal eye-sores of bamboo,
draped with striped polyester sheeting,
with attached bilingual plea:
"This shelter is meant to protect
"early morning walkers
"from the rain.
"Please do not destroy";

The small rocky stream, with its few mosquitoes
whining overhead;

Junior Police Call's experimental garden,
where enthusiasm waxed and waned;

A commercial garden;

Occasional snakes;

The wooden bench, one plank missing,
which—over a period of years—
we saw gradually reduced to a few, sad, damp, sticks;

Pylons straddling the paths;

Steep sections, where useful handholds going up
became treacherous roots going down;

Music, firecrackers, barking dogs, revving engines
from a village, "down there",
which we would have loved to visit,
but dared not intrude;

Sweaty fire-fighters marching down the hill,
at the end of a long day's work.
"We have to walk up to the fire," they told us,
"There's no other way to get there";

20

The black hill-side, remembrance of some person's
previous carelessness (not to say, "arson");

The middle-class walker with his faithful dog,
who said to us, one day, sadly,
when we asked, "Where's your dog?"
"I am going to tell you something
"you may not want to hear:
"he died";

The Philippines young man,
sitting on a chunam-plastered slope, at dusk,
facing the valley; not completely alone,
attentive to his bible, singing some hymns aloud,
with his master's labrador resting nearby.

21

Mythical Creatures[2]

"I've never been a ghost or a ghoul before",
the small girl said,
"nor a witch nor a werewolf!"—

So excitedly, she spoke,
gazing longingly
at the horrid ugly masks in a store,
some days before Hallowe'en!

But I'm sure she's been a sweetheart,
a good girl and an angel,
once or twice at least:

all, creatures that her parents
must sometimes think
are equally mythical!

22

Passing beauty (salon-wards):
Caged Jaguar and free spotted girl[3]

Your beautiful spots
and willingness
to take a photo call
almost made me late
to remove
my un-beauty spots
today.

23

Ambiguous Communication: Crossing the road to the Library[4]

I stand on the pedestrian bridge,
crossing over
between Victoria Park and the new library;
considering the route home.

I look for the bus that I plan to catch,
to see where it stops;
I stand for a minute or two,
a small trolley-bag in my hand,
gazing out over the road and the pavement below.

"Are you sure you want to go?"
a fellow pedestrian asks, in English;
not his mother tongue.

What did he mean? Did he fear
I might be thinking of suicide?

Or did he simply mean, "Don't you know
"where to go?", intending to offer help?

Or maybe again (thinking I would take a plane
and fly away), he was asking me to reconsider,
and stay?

24

David at Tai Po market KCR station[5]

"Hello", we said to each other,
quite intimately, as equals.

"Where are you going?" he asked,
looking at my two black trolley bags,
parked at my seat.

"Nowhere", I said. "I just always carry many things."
"Where've you come from?" he tried again,
aware of the obvious alternative.

"Nowhere", I answered again, "from home".

But he was concerned and fingered
my partly open zip, pulling it closed.
"You be careful!
"Someone may put their hand in
"and take something out."

"Thank you", I said.

But he was still concerned. He came back.
"I've heard that, in China,
"if you're on a bike, people will cut off
"your hand for the watch. You be careful!"

"Thank you for your concern", I said. "I will."

He smiled with youthful benevolence and went back
to his menial chores.

His physique, good English, and easy confidence
with me, a non-Chinese,
suggest he has lived in some kindly institution,

25

run by altruistic English-speakers.

His intelligence suggests otherwise.

Perhaps a job in MacDonald's is so desirable here,
that one feigns a modest simplicity, to get it?

26

Tai Po Lady[6]

It wasn't a bad journey. The rush hour
was over and I sat for some of the way.
The connections were managed quite well.
No-one helped me, of course. And it was I,
who had to duck and weave
to avoid the others;
not to hurt their toes or their legs.

I came to an escalator,
and stood, measuring its speed,
judging when to step on.

Several pushed past,
disturbing my planned rhythm.

But then a true Tai Po lady stepped up,
saw my dilemma and offered to help.

~~~

What a difference fellow-feeling can make!

Before memory fades, let me put on record,
that she began to make my day!

27
~~~

Seen in Shanghai[7]

In this current of—some separate,
some loosely grouped—pedestrians,
they make an eye-catching,
throat-catching couple:

the diffident, self-effacing mother,
with downcast eyes,
finding unbearable our curiosity,
maybe also, fearing our contempt;

son with straight-ahead glance,
proud of his achievements.

She holds his hand,
but I think he thinks
he's holding hers.

A Down's syndrome child
rarely makes thirty birthdays,
so books say. But he looks older.

Of course she loves him.
But her careful love
has multiplied her cares.

Prolonging his affectionate life,
she prolongs the death
of personal life
his birth inevitably
brought her;
beyond what mothers
usually endure.
If—no, when—he leaves her,
will her memories of him
and consciousness

28

she did all well—
her very best and more—
be strong enough
to help her hatch
out of the chrysalis
she shut herself inside;

cocooned from our interest,
cocooning him
from too much knowledge
of himself?

Will her own butterfly
unfold its wings then;
at last take to the vivid air?

29

30

2007

31

32

Public Secrets at the Post Office[8]

Writing a letter in the Post Office,
with your heart in your face
and at the top of your pen,

you unknowingly make public
the secrets of your soul.

33

A Relative Quiet at Yam O[9]

Today
a relative quiet strikes us
at Yam O.

A single mynah bird
calls out
from the top of a lamp-post.

A single careful plane moans unseen
behind the dreadful smog.

The buttercup trees glow
wordlessly,
with what we may suppose
is welcome.

And the flame trees
hold their fire.

The constant quiet lull of
Disney musak
transforms
the dirty air
to a screen
for mystery.

34

Wisdom at a Concert
Meeting a Meet Applause
or Concerted Wisdom[10]

Following a performance of a Tchaikovsky programme by the Moscow Philharmonic Orchestra, on Wednesday, 28 February 2007

Sitting here in Hong Kong—
crammed in plush green seats,

made to measure
by some latter-day Procrustes,
for persons of a smaller size
than we from Europe;
ignoring even the needs
of our tall neighbours from the North—

we are attentive to the Moscow Philharmonic,
and Yuri Simonov,
their elegantly groomed conductor;
who dances on the podium,
embracing the players with his distant arms,
throwing his expressive hands out
across the small space
that separates him from them.

He makes us laugh with pleasure;
we, sitting in our seats,
catching his exuberant enjoyment.

And when violinist, Boris Belkin,
concludes his competent performance
of Tchaikovsky's complex and difficult
Violin Concerto in D major—
so enchantingly and achingly romantic—

35

Yuri jumps off the podium,
embraces him, and
lands him two smackers,
one on each cheek.

"How wonderfully you played!"
he clearly feels. "How pleased I am with you!
"How I enjoyed your playing; my dancing
"along with your music,
"as your fingers danced
"and your arms moved strongly and swiftly
"rather than rhythmically,
"rendering quite marvelously
"the delicious and divine
"sounds the composer conceived
"a century and a quarter ago."[11]

The praise Yuri pours on the artist,
the artist extends to his instrument.
He bears his violin high in the air—
almost horizontal, in line with its bow—
as he sweeps off the stage,
sweeps out, and back, and out and back,
in the arms of our cascading applause;

modestly dressed,
—rather than consciously modishly—
in a bohemian style
that was common in the sixties:—
black T-shirt with black jacket
and trousers of dark and surprising blue.

Ever since I have known Hong Kong,
I have known what reputation
its audience bears;
demanding money's worth,
applauding and applauding,

36

hoping for encore after encore.

Tonight, I feel that this has changed.
The applause is still extreme, excited, hectic.
But for what cause?

Viewing the excitement
of the surely sophisticated
crowd; raising hands high as they clap
and clap and clap,
one thinks of masses in some vast public space,
shouting, "Heil Hitler!"; or hailing other leaders
who—similarly—possess
the gifts of demagoguery,
combined with fear-full opposition.
~~~
But back to the music.
~~~
The vastest crowds typically agglomerate
for the music which is the least complex,
the least meaningful,
ultimately the least resonant.

As the excellence of the essence
of a created thing increases,
becomes more specialized,
more complex,
its admirers thin out,

until we find it is one on one.
~~~
One appreciative soul exists
for the very best we have to offer.

What music we hope to play for him or her!
And how silent is the most appreciative applause.
~~~

Ferris wheel at night[12]

When we see a ferris wheel
at night,
lit up and shining,

we want to tell the screaming
fearing
crowds,
"It is this you are seeking,
"really:

"to be part of this
"bright colour—

"part of the divine light,

"made out of
"our chaos

"of inchoate sweat, motion, fear and noise".

38

Street Triptych[13]

A baby sucks his thumb for comfort.

A mother embraces her mobile phone for convenience.

A man consumes a cigarette,

with the utmost lascivious passion of all.

39

Gangways[14]

Watching the gangway raised
on to the ferry departing for DB,
peering through the narrowing, closing, gap,
and wondering if I'd catch sight of my husband,
hurrying, to be left behind,
and what I'd feel if I did;

with a catch of the heart,
I thought of those fleeing
some terrible danger,
some desperate political,
social, natural disaster;
seeing their loved ones
left behind.

How infinitely greater their pang of loss;
knowing suddenly
that separation is happening!

What a chasm
separates
the virtual certainty
of a very close reunion
from the agony of perceiving possibly final loss.

From such felt experiences
of our own,
we glean sharp glimmers of lives
much differently fortunate
but emotionally the same.

40

The Smell of Germolene[15]

The smell of germoline
percolated
through the air-conditioned
air of Bus E22, emanating
from the beginning-to-be-bald
Chinese gentleman ahead.

Germs do it. Presumably
not fighting their way
onto crowded trams, buses,
subway systems, trains, or
even planes; easily riding
both air and the struggling,
warm, incubating human flesh,
blood, hair, sloughing
skin, hair combings, nail
clippings, nose blowings
(pickings, dare one say, and the
products of pickings rolled into balls
and surreptitiously flicked away),
sneezes, coughs,
and noisy, fruity spits.

Germ-combating Germolene
and other more sophisticated
fighters of disease
—blasters, we would hope—
also travel continents. But
they have to pay their way;
consequently emerge slowly, make
their way selectively
and need our help
to help them help us
survive and thrive.

41

Can we help them a little?

Cover our mouths when we cough,
wash our hands (not too quickly),
wear a mask when infectious,
do not swim when carrying skin disease:—
things like that.

We all know what to do!

42

Microphone[16]

The Procrustes bed of
the microphone!

It fits only
the announcer
and imposes a character-test
on all performers who follow her!

Will they
seek to work
within
the unnecessary constraints
she has pre-set?

Or
insist
that
they
need
some consideration
too?

43

Familiarity[17]

People like familiarity:
the train stations they know
the same distant view
the cakes in the cake shop
the signature tune;
patterns on carpets, in quilts,
in marvelous baroque music,
in pages of poetry.

—They like sameness *more* than novelty, perhaps?—

Not sure if they do.

How about you?

44

Cornwall Road Garden[18]

The Gloria
English kindergarten and Primary School
sit sideways on
to a garden of plants,
schooled for decades at least
to form elephants and dinosaurs,
topiary pawns and blazing pergolas.

No forsaken garden this;

though the Chinese girl with her Caucasian lover
(almost furtively
eating a single lunch out of a takeaway box)
obviously thought it was more so, than it is,

and did not bargain for an English visitor,
with possibly enquiring camera;

and they cast their looks away and to the side.
~~~
The profusion of fertility here
is naked for who dares to see:—
thrusting stamens and pistils of hibiscus,
florets of bougainvillea, flowers of the palm.

And we can only suppose
the obscene innocence
of the children's playground toys
a deliberate attempt
to claim
the sexuality
is not here.



45
~~~

But two white butterflies
dance above each other in turns;
birds sing to attract
and call to summon their mates;

and even I sit creating a kind of life
in this unforgettable garden;
not so sidelined after all.

This children's superficial skewed world
(where fish are bigger than ponies
and even the toy clock points west)
is a surprisingly irreverent irrelevance.

The friendly panda gazes deeply
into your eyes.
The pachyderm extends his trunk. And
we see it is the knowing ram
(not the harmless lamb)
that offers us a ride.

No wonder adult supervision is advised.
And the children's swings double as scolds' bridles
(chastity belts too, doubtless, when the need is there).

A young woman, her eyes
tightly bound with green cloth,
—perhaps encouraging Marvell's
'green thought in a green shade'[19]—
sits immobile on a park bench,
waiting for something to happen.

46

Morrison 200th Anniversary Conference[20]

Celebrating the 200th Anniversary of the Reverend Robert Morrison's Arrival in China.

I look around the room and think:

All of you
were young men once:

bright, enthusiastic,
conscientious,
strong, talented and brave.

And you chose
a path that led you here.

Still
all those things.

But perhaps
a little tired.

47

Shooting Star *or* Heritage Hindered[21]

Written after demolition began of the original Star Ferry pier in Hong Kong and also after the related removal of ferry operations to another place; referring also to other current heritage matters. Although inspired by a specific action and specific statements in a single administrative region, this reflection is generally relevant.

We can all shoot ourselves in the foot
from time to time.
                    But self shooting
with a star is surely something rare?

"Civil Engineering *Destruction* Department",
the notice reads now;
"Development" changed by indignant young people,
asserting in bold graffiti, "It is wrong
"to destroy our history".

A strange statement, that. Can history be destroyed?

It happened. It has happened, then, for ever. Surely?

We cannot revisit what happened
before it happened
and prevent it, as in some
science fiction film.
Its consequences
will always survive,
ramifying like plant-life:
integrating with the present,
strangling some developments,

48

but also throwing up
lovely flowers of repentance,
forgiveness, inspiration.

We can remove signs of the past,
and more substantial survivals:
buildings, pathways,
places of arrival, departure,
joy and bitter loss.

We can destroy the records,
selectively cull them,
change the street names,
remove old letter-boxes,
well-meaningly pack away
the numbered stones,
to re-erect elsewhere;

permanently puzzling posterity.

If we obscure, cover, or destroy
the tracks previous people made,
we will change the impact of the past,
certainly.

And this will be added
to our history too.

Who knows
what our acts of omission and commission
will have caused,
when they also become history!

In the abandoned ferry forecourt,
where previously
touts accosted welcome tourists,
commuters queued for transport,

49

and news-vendors piled up
tomorrow's history,
a street person sits smiling,
his forearm resting on the street-art
cardboard cut-out sitter,
next to him,
perhaps his only friend.

Also here,
in the concrete ruins,
anxious old persons,
bereft of life-long habits, conveniences,
wander, complain.
~~~
But the wreckers
have their job to do.

The clock that told past time
is taken down, and stops.
Another—simulacrum of the past—is raised.

The old must adapt to changes.
The young will not know there have been any.

But, as a sop to the outcry,
virtual history is promoted now.
We can store pictures of the past,
video, film and digital files.
These we can have, we are told.

But how can these survive,
when more substantial things cannot?
Will not these be even easier
to scratch and bend?
~~~

In time, rejected, ignored, dismissed,
over-ridden, voted out,
like that lonely hugger of cardboard,
resting on his solitary comfort;

will we embrace our virtual history,

our Big Brother,

smiling, too?[22]

51

Fisherwoman: One: Ashes to Water[23]

On 7 April 2007, the first sea funerals were held in Hong Kong waters for city residents.[24]

"She loved the sea and often caught fish here",
her daughter said,
having cast the ashes to the waves.

"I felt her joy as I sent her back
"to where she was always happy.

"She wished me to do it.

"It was her last wish,
"which I have now fulfilled
"this Easter-tide.

"I think God wanted it too."

52

Fisherwoman: Two: She loved the Sea[25]

On 7 April 2007, the first sea funerals were held in Hong Kong waters for city residents.[26]

"She loved the sea and often caught fish here."

Yes, I suppose you would. Love it, I mean.
Familiarity can breed love.
And how could one work on the sea,
for hours, days, years, a lifetime,
and not like what one does?

A solitary fisher, perhaps. Thinking of the fish.

Focused on the water, the tides, wind and other weather.
Perhaps in the calm dwelling on self and family.

A Christian funeral, so a Christian lady.

A Christian family, it seems;
for her tearful daughter spoke of Easter
and God's Easter will.

To be a fisherwoman and a Christian too!

To hear the story of Christ's walk on water!

To know that the first disciples
whom Christ called
were fishermen too!

To know how He said to them,
"I will make you fishers of men"!

53

That, to one of them, Christ said,
"On this rock I will build my church".

To hear the story of the empty nets
miraculously filled.

The story of the loaves and the fishes
and the feeding of the five thousand.

How close she would feel to it all!

And, if she ever went to the town,
to the cathedral there,

saw the tribute to all fishers of fish
glowing in stained glass still,

how cherished she would feel,
perhaps;

or (if modest, as I think fisher-folk must be)
perhaps too much exposed.

But what would she make of the story
of the Gadarene swine?

Hearing how devils entered a herd of pigs,
who rushed to the edge of a cliff,
fell over, and drowned in the sea,

did she ever wonder
if there were devils
in the flotsam and jetsam
she must frequently
have increasingly seen
in the formerly clear deep waters;

54

always, once, reflecting the sky?

And, her ashes floating as her boat once did,
buoyant on the kindly rocking waves,
sinking down through the depths,
settling among the lobsters she used to catch,

will she be affronted
by harsh coloured plastic,
sharp tins and glass?

Or will she know
that the sea will redeem them too;

the movement of water on glass
take away its edge; rust, eat up the tin;
plastic (colonized by molluscs,
seaweed, and small shoals)
take on real life,
not merely dissemble it?

As for those in peril on the sea,

will she reflect

that all dangers are now
at an end

for her?

55

Communicable Smile[27]

A smile can be like pushing a button;
an action, producing
an equivalent reaction.

Walking down the street,
one day,
I flashed a bright smile
at a janitor,
standing in a doorway,
taking the air.

He was surprised,
briefly considered the phenomenon;
then, before I passed out of earshot,
called out, after me,
"Happy Easter!"—

A surprising greeting
in secular Hong Kong,
Buddhist Hong Kong,
Taoist Hong Kong,
but may be more
Christian Hong Kong
than I had realized before.

56

On the bus to Tuen Mun[28]

Half opening my eyes
on a Tuen Mun-bound bus,

I was amazed
at the largest arthurium
I'd ever seen;

I opened them wider,
and saw
an ordinary pink plastic bag,
hanging in a roadside crag.

Then came
Siu Lam Psychiatric Prison,

where a learned former judge
and his barrister wife
currently reside;

their former common sense,
wisdom and discretion
all lost or cast aside.

Next, rows of silver birches
naked in the hot sun,
their clothes of bark
scattered on the ground,
far and wide.

57

Five skulls at the window[29]

"Pak Oi Hospital Tuen Mun
Nursing Home",
I read from the bus,
passing by.

With a catch of the heart,
I see five skulls,
bleached white by the sun.

Five mops at the window.

58

Security unmanned[30]

The security post was unmanned, and
I wondered why. Then, as I
passed the podium, there,
I saw a group of eight guards,
engaged in the paradoxically
demoralizing exercise
of morning drill.

That friendly English-speaking
guard, whom I know quite well,
clearly considers standing up straight
not part of his job;

and most of them, perhaps,
consider the morning harangue
by an eager dame,
wearing the same
uniform
as themselves
not a worthwhile part of the game.

59

Applause: OR, A simply ambiguous life[31]

We clapped her life, not only her talk,
when it was over. This was my feeling.

Not that her talk didn't
come down the aisles to us
and tell us what we expected.

But her quiet self-possession
(doubtless built on great possessions),
her fairly direct confidences and confidence
(probably built on a life-time's protection)
warmed us to her gentle glow.

But oh yes, as someone said afterwards,
there was probably "much more to the lady"
than she was allowed to show.

And indeed, sitting not far from the front,
I heard her disappointed, short-lived protest,
as her interlocutor moved her on,
"But we've left an awful lot out!
"We've said nothing about [an unmentionable subject
now]."

And has that really been her story?
Not allowed to say what she wished.
Not allowed to initiate. Always,
required to respond to what others
had agreed she might be asked to do?
Always constrained by others' views
of what was appropriate for her?
Living in Shanghai as if it was Surbiton
(so she said),
Taught Philosophy in Bristol, in a way

60

old-fashioned even then
(so she said).
Marrying the man next door,
whom she met through his parents,
—her childhood patrons—
when he and she were both grown-up.
A fairy-tale in a way.

And then that big house in a posh
neighbourhood, with huge gardens
near a sandy beach, golf-club and much
quaint local colour. Charity work
of a mild type; a gracious figurehead
usefully encouraging other wealthy ladies
to shell out themselves and, in turn, to ask
their own less prominent contacts
to donate from their own lesser means.

And so she turns to her family. Perhaps
they will let her say what she thinks.
Her book, ostensibly for her grandchildren,
is, as she says, quite personal:
not for the general public,
where doubtless she places us all.

Why offer it us, then?
Surely, not for the few thousand dollars
you raise by this means
for two small children's charities,
when you control—or maybe only enjoy?—
so much opulence yourself?
Secretly, in your unrebellious
heart of hearts, is this
your way, at long last,
of telling us what you really think?

Or is there still very much more to tell?

61

Truth rules?[32]

There,

when the situation
the boss finds himself in
is difficult

and he lets others know
it is so,

they change the rules
to ease his path.

Here, too,

I find,
the boss says
whatever
he feels expedient;

even the truth,

sometimes.

62

Waving Goodbye[33]

Suddenly, I see them
standing at the door,
waving to us.

And I realize
they are moving further away
into the separateness
that death brings.

And I panic for a moment.

This is not what I want.

63

The flute-player: sweet and low[34]

The sweetness of his well-played tune
was lovely to hear. Lovely to see
was his seriousness.
                                        He sits low
on the ground; here, where we pass
thoughtlessly,
wordlessly,
ignoringly,
by.
But he has worked, sometimes,
as hard for mastery—musical, I mean—
as those we applaud from green plush seats,
comfortable, expensively bought;
calling for encore
after encore,
from the high stages,
where not only talent has put them.

His person is unobtrusive. He holds out
no hat or cup for alms. He offers none
of us his story, set out in pleading words,
begging our love.

He gives us what he has, without our asking for it.

Thank him for his gift.

But when you put a coin
carefully down to nestle
where his flute sleeps at night,
thank him with a smile
and some respectful words of praise.

He is an artist too and has his quiet pride.

64

Sipping Tea
at the Tea Museum, Hong Kong Park[35]

Whose lips rested here
—on the gilt scalloped bright bowl
on its small pedestal,
with the simple,
pink and blue, daisy dahlias,
improbable but effective?

Did she resemble
the two cheerful girls—
equally improbable perhaps
(as we view them today)—
gigglingly bending
across the curved slop-bowl
to gossip and exchange a joke or two,
resting in the fresh air,
in a stylised garden,
such as we can still find
in Asian places today?

Or was it rather a lady
of a different style,
hidden behind the windowed,
curtained wall nearby,
who sipped her days away
in patient idleness;
which these bright fantasies
slightly—ever so slightly—
lit up and made more tolerable?

65

"You can be like God"[36]

Awkwardly fixed, on a lamp-post
by the controlled crossing,
where usually the police affix notices,
seeking witnesses of fatal accidents,
is a prophet's message.

Some of us pause to read—in English or Chinese—
according to our taste, training, or ability,
his statement; then walk on, wondering
what family tragedy gave it voice.

"We are all in danger. Blameworthy
are the dangerous drivers, who do not
stop at the lights. If you drive carefully,
you can save a thousand lives.
You can be like God."

Such an exhortation to huge ego,
spiritual ambition and eschatological power!

—Could it work more
than the now standard,
stern, finger-wagging command,

"Do not drink and drive!"

66

Weather-vane[37]

Two birds perch on a high neon-lit lamp-post
facing different ways, Janus-like,
east and west.

That's OK.

Just as long as

one of them

doesn't turn

as a weather-vane does,

so both face the same way.

67

Double-take: recycled reading[38]

"Yes, the Chinese really respect reading!"
I thought, as I saw a down-and-out
with tangled long hair
and not very clean clothes
walk purposefully near
the pier, with quite a pile
of folded newspapers under his arm.

And I imagined him making for a quiet covered place
to read them.
But then I remembered the Government's
recycling campaign.

Should I have taken instead
the disappointingly cynical view
that his haste
was inspired—
not by love of literature—
but fear of confrontation;
having taken from a bin something
he meant not to read,
but to sell?

Then I looked around.

Sitting on a step, next to a notice,
headed, "Assistance: access to lower level",
was an elderly gentleman,
with gold-rimmed glasses
and sun spots,
reading a Chinese newspaper,
carefully folded at the place where he wanted to read.
His sandals were neatly placed at one side
and his feet rested, in red socks,

68

on another piece of newspaper.
He had a small plastic bag
containing other important belongings.

Seventy yards off, a young man sits in the sun,
also reading a newspaper.

And two other elderly gents, further off again,
sit companionably next to each other,
reading newspapers too.

I guess my first thought
was more right than wrong,
after all!

69

Beggarly Smile[39]

She smiled up at me
from the pavement
and I smiled back.

But my smile faltered,
partially froze,
when I saw
the large mug in her hand;
and the insincerity
of her apparent friendliness.

But I held my smile steady,
even as I thought, "She gives
"all she gets to the triads, who
"ask her to sit there".

And I smiled heartily again
when I thought, "At least
"I will give her a smile!

"That, I can happily give her;
"and, if she receives it,
"seeing what it is, its sincerity,
"that, at least, she can keep.

"The triads cannot
"take my smile
"away from her."

70

Patterns in a Garden Suburb[40]

I watched the little black girl,
with curly hair and woolly knitted cap,
on this, the first day of globally-warmed winter
in Hong Kong,
as she walked along the unbroken white line,
somehow, in the middle of the road; then
on the paradoxically less restrictive dotted line.

Would she move to the pavement
before the buses, that we waited for, came?

The next I saw, with her right foot
on the pavement and her left
in a presumably dry drain,
she was
continuing
her now jerky way to school.

Then a dog barked.—At her?
A little boy ran.—To her?

The first bus came.

Our relationship ended.

But these words will remember her
and also remind that patterns sustain,
rituals delight.

But the unexpected occurs,
jolting us
into the different worlds
that others perceive,
and their—often equally innocent—make-believe.

71

Torch the Nest Egg![41]

The moated egg floated in a green maze of shrubs.
The bird's nest spread across the land, like an ancient tumulus,
stripped to the skeletons of those who ran and jumped
and strove for excellence centuries ago;

as the water cube waited to reveal its depths
and the built torch waited for the touch
that would complete its lights.

But a countryman still raised his head
to gaze out, off a pedestrian footbridge,
at the bumper to bumper cars, motionless,
seemingly painted on the eight-lane highway;

a single labourer tipped building waste
from a simple wheelbarrow;

a single worker swung in a solitary gondola
racing at speed up the wall of the athletes' village;

and a group of three take a rest on the sloping glass
of another emerging building.

Not only the world's athletes are competing here;
a country's people has sacrificed and hoped;
a country's workers have experienced weariness and pain;
a country's leaders have taken thought.

Few athletes will win gold. For most
the praise received will be for taking part.

A censorious world may award few perfect scores.

72

But let us hope the Chinese people will be praised
for the will they show to practice for perfection.

Whichever of us is perfect will not cast a stone of
blame
for this.

73

Beijing in Blossom Time[42]

The vivid dark fuschia of flowering peach
stands rigid by the busy road
alert to the rare cyclist.

The soft petals of cherries
drift like soft silky snow
in the garden of the Friendship Hotel,

where
men in camouflage fatigues with spades for guns
(swords beaten to ploughshares, perhaps)
move large stones in broken heaps.
~~~
Inside the Capital Museum,

a replica
Nestorian Christian cross
rests on a Buddhist lotus;

and we also see
facsimiles of powerful papers—
treaties and declarations—

with two small chairs stripped of shine
beside a low carved table,
somewhat fragile from the passage of worms and time.

Examination cribs are displayed, sewn
into the conveniently-padded garments
that aspiring candidates wore
in imperial times;

and pre-Olympic souvenirs.
~~~
At lunch, the driver offered you beer

74

—the same brand that won the Olympic concession.—
And we mime that it will surely give you strength
to perform strong acts of unusual athleticism.

"You drive very well", you pleasantly said.
And he replied, "It's my work.
"If I didn't drive well, I would lose my job."

75

Breakfast time at the Friendship Hotel[43]

Willow cotton
rolls in balls
as the long mop sweeps the floor.

Two men
swing
their arms in the brightening morning air.

A new welcome balloon
bounces above the ornate glass door.

Big bouquets
arrive,
and the conference bags.

Soon the sweet-faced artist with the brown curls
will sit
in the long corridor and
paint
flowers and birds and trees that few
will buy,
receiving her smile for free.

OTHER POEMS

2007 and 2008

77

78

Rose-petals: Dali and Carroll[44]

After seeing Salvador Dali's sculpture of the fictional character, Alice, the central character in two stories by "Lewis Carroll" (the pen-name of Oxford mathematician, Charles Dodgson).

Dali's Alice has no features on her face,
just rose petals
where eyes, nose, mouth, ears, should be; reflecting,
so the caption says, her innocence,
her pre-adult ignorance of life.
And the skipping-rope above her head,
it tells us too, doubles as the looking glass,
through which she slipped into a fancy world
of fantasy.

—But the fantasy was Charles's,
not her own?—

Dali's rose petals belie the sharp
intelligence that Dodgson gave his Alice—
scornful of his adult toys
(Tweedledee and Tweedledum,
Humpty Dumpty, the Red Queen,
the old man sitting on a gate)—
yet still casually comforting
the adult woes they seemingly felt.

Two great eccentrics,
one drawing on
the other's work,

yet producing so apparently opposite a vision.
One conceiving innocence

79

to lie in ignorance—
possible through undeveloped
carnal knowledge; so to speak,
absence of the tools for sensual experience,
absence of experiences too, therefore.

But the other
reported innocence quite differently.

His Alice lives adult experiences,
understands what they are,
sees them sharply, but scornfully.
Sees, hears, smells, tastes and swallows them.

Her rose petals are hidden elsewhere.

The quiet Oxford don, with his penchant
for taking photographs
of nude young girls,
pries through to the hidden
nature of natures;

while the flamboyant Catalan grandee
manipulates
their surface features.

80

Tengmalm's (Funeral) Owl[45]

The light was poor in the early afternoon,
up there in Scotland's highland north,
as we drove to the stone cairns, eager
to see what was there.

The quality of light
gave more the impression
of absence of sun,
than anything in our previous experience;
not simply reflecting the time of day:
suggested indeed
that there never
was any sun up there, at all.

The cairns were easy to find:
each a careful smallish pile of stones,
a bit like an igloo.

You played a man's part;
led the way and crawled inside
to see what was there, what it was like.

"Find out for yourself!"
you said, when you emerged
and I asked the obvious question.

Fearfully,
I placed my head and shoulders
in through the opening

and experienced

nothing.

Nothing.

81

No presences. No ghosts from the past.
No anger at intrusion. No overwhelming sorrow, felt
for their long separation from life.
No joy at the solace that our company—
however briefly—brought.

Nothing battened on the fresh blood
of our warm pulses
or our cheeks, reddened by the summer's cold.

I guess they were too far distant from us.

Distant in time.

But also in their thoughts;
in their preoccupations.

There was nothing in us
that they recognized
(in that brief space of time,
when we were there)
that they could use as a platform
to build communication on.

The tuning fork of our apprehensions
may have struck on their dust,
compacted with the stones
where they still may have sheltered
from their Neolithic times.

But we could not hear
the sound they made, thus struck,
far less, distinguish the key
in which their resonances spoke.

It was a strongly absent experience
of nothing;

82

powerful enough
to emerge thousands of miles away,
eighteen years on,
on a hot Sunday afternoon
of blazing sun,
here in Hong Kong;

where ancestors are closely felt
and cherished,
held tight within the family.
~~~
Have you finally
found a way to talk to us,
after all?

I must ponder what you are seeking to say.
The line may be open now,
but no message has come through,
yet.
~~~
I think back again:

to the straight narrow road
across a flat, bare, grassed landscape,
with no distant view;

the absence of light
intensifying
as we returned from the non-experience
of our visit;

and to the sudden astonishing epiphany
of a small owl,
sitting on a low wire, skirting the road;
its soft, pale-cream feathers,
interspersed with pale brown,

83

reflecting the dipped headlights of our slow hire-car,
bumping up from a slight dip,

as we returned to the hotel;

with its unnecessary five-course early dinner,
poorly-acting, purple-coloured jacuzzi
and morning newspapers received in the mid
afternoon.

84

Knowing her Name[46]

You sew them in
when they go into the nursing home.

And then
you remove them
when their last
earthly garment
is discarded
with them.

But this last time,
I—her only daughter, only child;
herself an only child,
widow of an only son—
let it be,
clearly sewn and shown on the manufacturer's label.

Then the people who sort it,
look at it, try it,
buy it and wear it,

will see her name,
and wonder what she was like,
the person
who wore this before.

And someone else
will then know her name.

85

Penates[47]

Approaching
our regular holiday home,
I wonder where
my underclothes are.

I remember
that small piece of furniture
from Hong Kong;

and feel at home again,
in imagination.

And I remember
that advice from a women's periodical:
"Always carry with you,
when you travel,
something to bond you
to where you are travelling to:
a photograph; a picture; a small ornament".

Such good advice.

And then I remember,
this is what the Trojans
did too.

Fleeing the Greeks,
"et dona ferentes",
and their destructive equine gift
(wooden but potent, soon to be in flames)—
which stubborn and misguided priests
saw as offered in religion's name—
they took with them their "Penates",
their household gods;

86

something to remind them
where they came from;

to recall their roots, their culture,
their lost dear ones:

seeds for a future
without and beyond them;

in some small way built on them;
in some small way continuing them;

carrying them, too,
into the limitless future
of a new world.

87

Word-diggers[48]

Thoughts on research, writing and publishing, partly suggested by the failed intellectual property case that Michael Baigent and Richard Leigh brought, claiming that Dan Brown's novel, "The Da Vinci Code", copied their own book "Holy Blood, Holy Grail" (1982).[49]

We word-diggers labour like slaves
in the closeted, cold, lonely—often dirty—
depths of the elemental mine of the world's words.

The gold is there. We see its dull shine
and even dig it out from time to time,

shoveling it out

(still firmly embedded
in the hard rock,
where it has lain for years)

onto the wheeled trucks
that carry it to the air.

There, others—high artists—
extract it from the dross, polish it,
mould it to fine objects of high price,
acknowledge us not at all.

But the first work was ours.
We found the gold; it was we,
who separated it from what
was less important,
understanding its potential.
Others knew its nature
only after we nosed it out,

88

isolated it, smelt its quality.

We acknowledge their creative work,
of course. But in our hearts,
we feel—considering their place in life—
if roles reversed,
we could do their work;

but partly doubt
they could tolerate ours;

given its laborious nature
and the nature of its laboriousness.

As for more popular writers,
they need our gold
to melt, pour and mould
for the people's taste.

It is our gold then, often,
that publishers coin,
passed up to them by agents,
editors and familiar friends,

which in due course returns to them again,
circulating through bookshops,
websites, launch parties and all
the many activities
that produce more funds
for ever much more popular publishing;

swallowing up
the gold we word-slaves
find and treasure,

happy to be the pioneers,
the seekers for value and beauty;

89

but perhaps not entirely happy
not to be acknowledged
by those who pocket the cash;

not entirely happy that a small percentage,
at least, isn't thrown our way, now and then.

90

Caring Professionals[50]

"Those who cure you will kill you!"[51]
What would we have made of this,
this occult, dark and threatening forecast,
if someone said it to us?

Certainly, it would puzzle us.

And then, whenever it happened—
days, weeks, months, years later—
that, allegedly, eight medical professionals
failed to kill hundreds
of the British public
whom they were paid to cure,
it would have come back to us
with the staggering comprehension
of hindsight.
~~~
But now we know what may have happened,
we must concentrate and think,
from what group
the next traitors will be drawn;

consider who will be the next
clever, well-trained, political idiots,
to attack us from within;

and the answer comes so easily,

our priests, of course:
taught to forgive, to love,
to turn the other cheek,
doubtless appalled at war,
death, politics, turmoil,
dishonesty and deceit.



91
~~~

Wouldn't it be easy
for a Moslem imam
—one of those who teaches
packed congregations
to support war, encourage resistance,
and to hate,
unmitigated by any thought
of circumstance or cultural relativity—

Wouldn't it be easy,
for such a man,

to turn a Christian priest (persuasion immaterial)
to pity the Moslem cause,
and pitying, to assist it?

Terrorism and thought control[52]

When I think of all the experiences
that meet, merge, and prompt
words and ideas,

and all the experiences
that others have had too,

it makes me quite giddy.

How can we ever control terrorism

by seeking to control

what others think?

93

Blogs (Web logs)[53]

Apparently such an innovation!—
baring one's thoughts to the universe
of souls, willing to read what one writes.

But is it so different?

Some diaries
were always written, with an eye
to the reader.

And in fact,

quite a bit
is pretty much the same;

modeled on what already exists:—

the newspaper column, the book and theatre review,
the fashion page, gossip column, etcetera.

And not only this, computers themselves
—and their software—echo
previous structures;

with their different levels
of memory; their operating systems, folders and files;
the ability to undo, destroy, restart and rethink.

Indeed, it seems all human tools,
all inventions, begin
with observation
of what already is.

Sometimes our bodies give the clue.
~~~

94
~~~

For a hose-pipe, a hinge, a grab;
penis, elbow and hand surely set the tone.

As for thinking up a standard measure;
span, foot and cubit
showed the way.

As for transforming raw matter
into energy or fuel,
leaving waste behind;
what closer model can there be
than eating, acting, achieving,
followed by sweat, urination, defecation?
~~~

We are all shaped by the structures
we have lived with.

Encountering other cultures,
we feel disorientation and dismay.

95
~~~

Anthropological Museum[54]

Man invented Christianity,
made God lose his son,
so God would understand
the pain such losses give
and treat man better after that.

96

Image[ination][55]

Some say that man was made
in the image of God.

Is it not rather that God was made
in the image of man?

Vengeful, intolerant,
jealous, angry,
paternal[istic]?

97

Imaginary Existence[56]

When you think about a person—

what they are,
skilled, experienced, loving and kind,

a synergy of every detail
they have seen, heard, felt, smelled, tasted,
said, and thought—

each of us
totally irreplaceable and yes
(in spite of what we say) indispensable—

and how we exist, only because and if
our heart pumps,
our lungs inhale and exhale,
our livers process,
our kidneys and intestines excrete,
our immune systems resist attack,

and if the environment sustains us—

it doesn't make sense.

No wonder
we have invented
immortality,

made a god die and live again,

to imagine *we* can,

too.

98

The Hukilau[57]

Came the time when the hula dancers
gave their only half-desired lesson to the crowd

and some of us stepped outside pretty fast,
not wanting to be chosen for the show

which we nevertheless wanted to see;

and one of us learnt the lesson so well,
that he internalized, interpreted it.

Asked to mime fishes, swimming in
the sea, and fishermen catching them,

he mimed his own culture's
variant sport—fly-fishing—

with neat,
ninety percent serious,
ten percent humorous
aplomb;

as he moved his feet to the right,
to the right, to the left, to the left,
and on, so on,

—aloha!—mahalo!—well done!

99

Pollarded:
Frank Coluccio Construction[58]

The trumpet tree
wears a black band,
in mourning for its lopped limbs.

—"If thy limb offend you,
cut it off."—

But should we sacrifice
the healthy growth of another's limbs,
even if that other is a tree?

100

Stop Requested[59]

The pale pretty young woman
with fine honey-blonde hair
pulled up in a bun, carries
the base of her baby's pram.

The dark young man—her partner
at least—carries the part
containing the baby.

The girl gives no smile to her man.
but a faint occasional smile
at their baby.

I feel rather sorry for him.

101

Spirit and Sense[60]

If one had a child who died,

could one miss the smell of him,
the touch of him,

more than the spirit,

which does survive?

102

Cassandra[61]

Cassandra is the mother
all of us have.

Looking at stairs,
she sees her husband, father or son
fall, fracture, fragment;
and their and her future lives
disintegrate

with a single
ill-judged
step.

*

I have become the Cassandra
every wife and mother is.

Looking at stairs,
I see you or me or anyone
fall, fracture, fragment;
and our or their future lives
disintegrate

with a single
ill-judged
step.

103

Understanding Her[62]

As you become

your Mother,

gradually—and at last—

you understand her.

104

Leaving Clothes[63]

It's not a bad idea to leave one's clothes
and other types of thing—"the residue"—
to one's daughter.

Then for years to come
she will think,

"This was Mother's fresia-fragrant dusting powder.
"How nice she smelt!" Or,
"What fashionable lip-stick Mother chose!
"What good quality lingerie she wore!"

And the numerous frilly nightgowns
will recall
the many ordered operations,
she underwent
quite bravely.

105

Concerns[64]

As you walk haltingly across the bridge
that we bouncily consume with sprightly tread,
do you feel shame, resentment;
feel bitter, envious perhaps?
Or—generously—do you enjoy
the prominent mobility we others display?

And you (the other, shorter, round gentleman,
with beads in your fists),
what do you worry about?
What do you pray for?
—Yourself?—
Or the sadness and joys
of our world?

106

Cat-calls[65]

"Cats don't really know their name",
my dead dear friend said.
"They just know their tone of voice.
"'Henry!'", she called—to demonstrate—
in Gladstone's tone of voice, her point.

And her belovèd black cat looked up,
knowing he was called.

By accident, just now, I eureka-ed a related fact.
Door-entry systems act the same as cats!

With confidence, forgetting where I was,
I punched my code for my work xerox-machine.

And—"open sesame!"—my front door opened before
me.

107

Sukhothai[66]

The absence
of a clearly perceived presence
implies existence.

108

Pumpkin man[67]

His skin is thin
as an onion's;
taut as lantern paper.

From his featureless
pumpkin face,
his eyes peer out,
all-seeing.

We fear to meet those eyes,
to find the emotions behind
his horrific, horrifying,
destroyed mask of a face.

He lies there on the walkway,
uncomfortably prone,
cap gesturing for him
for alms.

But at the end of the day
(one may see, if the timing is right),
he has a home to return to;
stands up,
puts his cap on his head,
walks away.

109

110

Notes

[1] Hong Kong, Experienced 1992-2003, edited from notes, 2006.
Johnny Appleseed is the nickname of the American John Chapman (1776-1845 (or 1847)), who planted apple-trees, was kind to animals, and dressed humbly, giving better clothes to the needy. He was a traveler all his life who never settled down with wife and home. The Walt Disney film segment, "The Legend of Johnny Appleseed", was made in 1948.
[2] Hong Kong, November 2006.
[3] Hong Kong, October or November 2006.
[4] Hong Kong, Autumn, 2006, revised July 2007.
[5] MacDonald's, Tai Po KCR station, New Territories, Hong Kong, 22 October 2006.
[6] Tai Po KCR station, Hong Kong, 22 October 2006.
[7] Shanghai, December 2006. First published in IMPRINT 2009: the Annual Anthology of the Women in Publishing Society, Hong Kong.
[8] Hong Kong, 2007.
[9] Hong Kong, 16 February 2007.
[10] Hong Kong, Experienced 28 February 2007, written 1 March 2007.
Procrustes is a character in a Greek story. He gave hospitality to travellers but insisted they had to fit the bed he offered them. This he achieved for them, either by lopping of parts of those who were too tall for the bed or stretching those who were too short for it.
[11] Tchaikovsky's only concerto for violin was premiered in 1881.
[12] Hong Kong, February/March 2007.
[13] Hong Kong, c. 1 March 2007.
[14] Hong Kong, March 2007.
[15] Hong Kong, March 2007.

111

---

[16] Hong Kong, March 2007.
[17] Hong Kong, March 2007.
[18] Hong Kong, 26 March 2007.
[19] Andrew Marvell, English 17th metaphysical century poet, wrote a wonderful poem, called, 'The Garden', discussed by William Empson in *Seven Types of Ambiguity*, in which the final lines conclude a mystical experience, 'annihilating all that's made to a green thought in a green shade'.
[20] Hong Kong, Notes made 26-28 April 2007. Written up 11 June 2007.
[21] Hong Kong, Written April 2007. Seen some weeks earlier.
First published in *Imprint 2008*: the Annual Anthology of the Women in Publishing Society, Hong Kong. Now revised.
[22] In the final scene of George Orwell's dystopian novel, *1984*, the anti-hero, Winston Smith, declares that he loves Big Brother, the symbol of the totalitarian state of which he is a citizen. Orwell presents this as a tragedy far greater than Smith's anticipated later execution will be. Winston Smith's job, as a member of the intelligencia, has previously been to rewrite or destroy the historical record, as appropriate, from time to time, to changing political circumstances.
[23] Hong Kong, April 2007.
[24] Loretta Fong, 'Ashes of 11 scattered in first sea funeral', SCMP, 8 April 2007, 'National'. According to this article, waters off Tap Mun, Tung Lung Chau, the West Lamma Channel and The Brothers (near Lantau) have been designated by the Government for the casting of ashes.
[25] Hong Kong, April 2007.
[26] Loretta Fong, 'Ashes of 11 scattered in first sea funeral', SCMP, 8 April 2007, 'National'. According to this article, waters off Tap Mun, Tung Lung Chau, the

---

West Lamma Channel and The Brothers (near Lantau) have been designated by the Government for the casting of ashes.
In this poem there are several references to the Gospels in the Christian Bible, as follows: the story of the Gadarene swine (e.g. Matthew 8: 30-32); "on this rock I will build my church" (e.g. Matthew, 6: 18); the story of the feeding of the five thousand (e.g. John, 6: 1-4); the calling of the first Apostles (e.g. Matthew, 4: 18-22); Christ walking on water (e.g. Matthew, 14: 22-33).
[27] Hong Kong, Easter (7 April) 2007.
[28] Hong Kong, Observed 12 May 2007, completed 21 May 2007.
[29] Hong Kong, Observed 12 May 2007, completed 21 May 2007.
[30] Hong Kong, 16 May 2007.
[31] Hong Kong, 28 May 2007.
[32] Hong Kong, 7 June 2007.
[33] July 2007.
[34] Hong Kong, September 2007. First published in the English Speaking Union (Hong Kong) on-line Newsletter, 2007.
[35] Hong Kong, 20 September 2007.
[36] Hong Kong, 3 November 2007.
[37] Hong Kong, 8 November 2007.
[38] Hong Kong.
[39] Hong Kong.
[40] Hong Kong, 14 January 2008.
[41] Beijing, 16, 17, 18 April 2008. Written during a visit to Beijing, shortly before the 29th Summer Olympics were to take place the same summer. It was at the time that protests about China's Tibet policy were causing the Dalai Lama dismay and China's spokesmen were reacting angrily and defensively.

Stunning new buildings erected for, or to

coincide with the Beijing Olympics have contrastingly homely nicknames. The new National Theatre for the Performing Arts in Beijing is 'The egg'. The National Aquatics Centre is 'The water cube'. And the National Stadium is 'the bird's nest'. The Beijing National Stadium was opened to the press for the first time on Wednesday 16 April (a mere couple of months behind schedule) and hosted its first event, a 'Good Luck Beijing' walk, on Friday 18 April. The new National Theatre for the Performing Arts opened in December 2007, three or so years plus behind schedule, after more than forty years in the planning. While we were in Beijing (11-17 April 2008), a North Korean opera troupe was performing a show reportedly featuring oppressive landlords and sturdy peasants. The National Aquatics Centre, begun on the same day as the Bird's Nest, was completed earlier; handed over for use on 28 January 2008.

On 16 April, when we visited them, the bird's nest was drawing a constantly renewing crowd of interested Chinese and some foreigners. The Water Cube, a short distance away as the crow flies, was also a popular draw. A group of senior citizens crowded at the flimsy barrier a couple of hundred yards from the building, pointing and looking over at it, eagerly.

Very close is another Olympic building then also nearing completion, the tall tower building, shaped like a flaming Olympic torch.

The cost of the Bird's Nest was tremendous: 3.5 billion yuan ($500.7 million). The human cost was great too. 4,707 residents were relocated from 2,043 households in the surrounding area. (Thomson Reuters 18 April 2008, 'FACTBOX — Five Facts about Beijing's Bird's Nest')

Norman Foster (Lord Foster) designed the new Beijing Airport, the biggest in the world which opened

29 January 2008. Travellers from Hong Kong will find familiar elements.

[42] Beijing, April 2008.

[43] Beijing, 17 April 2008.

[44] Hong Kong, April 2007.

[45] North East Scotland, 15 April 2007 (from notes made some days earlier). First published in IMPRINT 2009: the Annual Anthology of the Women in Publishing Society, Hong Kong.

We stayed the night of 22 August 1989 in Lybster (Portland Arms Hotel) and visited the Camster cairns, dating, it is said, from c. 2,000 BC, the 'hill of stanes' (250 small stones) and the 'standing stanes'. Details retrieved by reference to Verner Bickley's series of holiday notebooks and my own catalogue of photographs.

The Hotel had a named picture of an owl, very similar to the owl we saw, and this is how we know that what we saw was a Tengmalm's Owl. There is much information on the web about this type of owl, also known as 'Aegolius funereus', for example in a page compiled by Deane P. Lewis, 'OwlPages.com Owl Species ID: 230.010.000 - Page last updated 2005-04-25', at: http://www.owlpages.com/owls.php?genus=Aegolius&species=funereus

[46] Andorra, July 2007.

[47] Andorra, July 2007.

[48] Andorra, Summer 2007.

[49] See online article from CNN in London, dated 7 April 2006.

[50] Andorra, 7 July 2007.

[51] An Anglican clergyman, in Iraq (if I remember correctly), interviewed on British TV after the failed car bomb attacks in London and Glasgow, in early July 2007, said he had a conversation with a Moslem

115

extremist, who said this to him.
[52] Andorra, July 2007.
[53] Andorra, 7 July 2007.
[54] Mexico City, 14-17 August 2007.
[55] Mexico City, 14-17 August 2007.
[56] Mexico City, 14-17 August 2007.
[57] Honolulu, 24-30 August 2007.
[58] Honolulu, 24-30 August 2007. 43 And if thy hand offend thee, cut it off: it is better for thee to enter into life maimed, than having two hands to go into hell, into the fire that never shall be quenched.
45 And if thy foot offend thee, cut it off: it is better for thee to enter halt into life, than having two feet to be cast into hell, into the fire that never shall be quenched.
47 And if thine eye offend thee, pluck it out: it is better for thee to enter into the kingdom of God with one eye, than having two eyes to be cast into hell fire. (Gospel of Saint Mark, Christian Bible, King James translation, Chapter 9, verses 43, 45, 47.)
[59] Honolulu, 24-30 August 2007.
[60] 3 November 2007.
[61] Hong Kong.
[62] Hong Kong, 2007. First published in *Imprint 2008*: the Annual Anthology of the Women in Publishing Society, Hong Kong.
[63] Hong Kong.
[64] Hong Kong, seen 28 May 2008, written 29 May 2008?
[65] Andorra, Summer 2008. From previous notes.
[66] Andorra, Summer 2008.
[67] Hong Kong, November 2008.

116

ABOUT THE AUTHOR

GILLIAN BICKLEY, born and educated in the United Kingdom, has lived mostly in Hong Kong since 1970. Her poetry collections include “For the Record and other Poems of Hong Kong” (2003, 2016), “Moving House” (2005, 2016), “Sightings” (2007, 2016), “China Suite” (2009, 2016) and “Perceptions” (2012, 2016). Two collections, “Moving House” and “For the Record”, have been published in Chinese; individual poems have been translated into several languages, including Arab, Czech and Turkish and anthologised in Hong Kong, the Philippines, Romania and the United Kingdom. In July 2014, at the 18th International Festival, “Curtea de Arges Poetry Nights”, held in Romania, she was awarded the “Grand Prix Orient-Occident Des Arts” by the Festival Board and in 2016, a bilingual (English/Romanian) collection of her poems was published in Romania. She is one of the Hong Kong poets discussed in Agnes S. L. Lam's study, “Becoming poets: The Asian English Experience”.

Her other writings include “The Golden Needle: The Biography of Frederick Stewart (1836-1889)” (1997) and “The Stewarts of Bourtreebush” (2003). She is the editor of “Hong Kong Invaded! A ’97 Nightmare” (2001), “The Development of Education in Hong Kong, 1841-1897” (2002), “A Magistrate’s Court in Nineteenth Century Hong Kong: Court in Time” (2005, 2009), and “The Complete Court Cases of Magistrate Frederick Stewart” (2008). With Richard Collingwood-Selby, she co-edited “In Time of War” (2013) (the selected writings, photographs and drawings of Henry Collingwood-Selby).

A long-term adjudicator at the Hong Kong Schools’ Speech Festival, she was one of the Adjudicators for the Royal Commonwealth Society Hong Kong Poetry Writing Competition, and one of four voices in the full audio recording of Verner Bickley’s three volume anthology, "Poems to Enjoy". Her poems are popular with students and teachers for competitions, festivals and grade examinations.

Dr Bickley taught in the Department of English at the

117

Hong Kong Baptist University, as Senior Lecturer / Associate Professor, for twenty-two years. She has also taught at Universities in Lagos, Nigeria; Auckland, New Zealand; and the University of Hong Kong.

With her husband, Verner Bickley, she is co-founder of two international literary prizes, The Proverse Prize for unpublished writing and the Proverse Poetry Prize (single poems).

Elbert Siu Ping Lee, who contributes a Preface to "China Suite and other Poems", teaches psychology at the Hong Kong Campus of Upper Iowa University and is a member of the adjunct faculty. An occasional magazine contributor, he writes poems and feature articles. Some of his work can be found in *Asian Cha* and *Macao Poetry* (both online English literary and poetry magazines). Recently published poems appear in *Hong Kong Poems, an English-German anthology* (Stauffenburgs, 2007) and in *Fifty/Fifty: A new anthology of Hong Kong writing* (Haven Books, 2008). His first poetry collection, "Rain on the Pacific Coast", supported by Hong Kong Arts Development Council, was published by Proverse in 2013.

WRITE TO US!

We are interested to read **your** comments on
Gillian Bickley's *China Suite and Other Poems.*
Write to our email address, proverse@netvigator.com,
giving us a few sentences,
which you are willing for us to publish,
describing your response to this book.
If your comments are chosen to be included
in our E-Newsletter or website,
we will select another title published by Proverse
and send you a complimentary copy.
Please include your name, email address and mailing address
when you write to us, and state whether or not we may cut or
edit your comments for publication.
We will use your initials to attribute your comments.

118

ABOUT PROVERSE HONG KONG

Proverse Hong Kong is based in Hong Kong with expanding long-term regional and international connections.

Proverse has published novels, novellas, fictionalized autobiography, non-fiction (including biography, diaries, history, memoirs, sport, travel narratives), single-author poetry collections, children's, teens / young adult and academic books. Other interests include academic works in the humanities, social sciences, cultural studies, linguistics and education. Some Proverse books have accompanying audio texts. Some are translated into Chinese.

Proverse welcomes authors who have a story to tell, wisdom, perceptions or information to convey, a person they want to memorialize, a neglect they want to remedy, a record they want to correct, a strong interest that they want to share, skills they want to teach, and who consciously seek to make a contribution to society in an informative, interesting and well-written way. Proverse works with texts by non-native-speaker writers of English as well as by native English-speaking writers.

The name, "Proverse", combines the words "prose" and "verse" and is pronounced accordingly.

119

THE PROVERSE PRIZE

The Proverse Prize, an annual international competition for an unpublished book-length work of fiction, non-fiction, or poetry, was established in January 2008. Unusually for a competition of this nature, it is open to all who are at least eighteen on the date they sign the entry form and without restriction of nationality, residence or citizenship.

The objectives of the Proverse Prize are: to encourage excellence and / or excellence and usefulness in publishable written work in the English Language, which can, in varying degrees, “delight and instruct”. Entries are invited from anywhere in the world. Semi-finalists to date include writers born or resident in Andorra, Australia, Canada, Germany, Hong Kong, New Zealand, Nigeria, Singapore, Taiwan, The Bahamas, the PRC, the United Arab Emirates, the United Kingdom, the USA.

Summary Terms and Conditions
(for indication only & subject to revision)

The information below is for guidance only. Please refer to the year-specific Proverse Prize Entry Form & Terms & Conditions, which are uploaded, no later than 14 April each year, onto the Proverse Hong Kong website: <www.proversepublishing.com>.

The free Proverse E-Newsletter includes ongoing information about the Proverse Prize.

To be put on the E-Newsletter mailing-list, email: info@proversepublishing.com with your request.

120

The Prize

1) Publication by Proverse Hong Kong, with

2) Cash prize of HKD10,000 (HKD7.80 = approx. US$1.00)

Supplementary publication grants may be made to selected other entrants for publication by Proverse Hong Kong.

Depending on the quality of the work in any year, the prize may be shared by at most two entrants or withheld, as recommended by the judges.

In 2016, the entry fee was: HKD220.00 OR GBP32.00.

Writers are eligible, who are at least eighteen on the date they sign The Proverse Prize entry documents. There is no nationality or residence restriction.

Each submitted work must be an unpublished publishable single-author work of non-fiction, fiction or poetry, the original work of the entrant, and submitted in the English language. School textbooks and plays are ineligible.

Unpublished first translations into English (including those already published in the writer's mother tongue) submitted by the author are welcome. The submitted work will not be judged as a translation but as an original work.

Extent of the Manuscript: within the range of what is usual for the genre of the work submitted. However, it is advisable that novellas be in the range 30,000 to 45,000 words); other fiction (e.g. novels, short-story collections) and non-fiction (e.g. autobiographies, biographies, diaries, letters, memoirs, essay collections, etc.) should be in the range, 75,000 to 100,000 words. Poetry / poetry collections should be in the range, 5,000 to 25,000 words. Other word-counts and mixed-genre

121

submissions are not ruled out.

Writers may choose, if they wish, to obtain the services of an Editor in presenting their work, and should acknowledge this help and the nature and extent of this help in the Entry Form.

The regulations are updated from time to time. Please visit proversepublishing.com for updated entry information.

KEY DATES FOR THE PROVERSE PRIZE IN ANY YEAR

(subject to confirmation and/or change)

Receipt of Entry Fees / Entry Documents	[No later than] 14 April to 31 May of the year of entry
Receipt of entered manuscripts	1 May to 30 June of the year of entry
Cash Award Made	At the same time as publication of the work(s) adjudged the winner / joint-winners of the Proverse Prize
Publication of winning work(s)	In or after November of the year that follows the year of entry

122

WINNERS OF THE PROVERSE PRIZE WHOSE ENTERED WORK HAS ALREADY BEEN PUBLISHED BY PROVERSE HONG KONG

Rebecca Tomasis
Laura Solomon
Gillian Jones
David Diskin
Peter Gregoire
Sophronia Liu
Birgit Linder
James Mccarthy
Philip Chatting
Celia Claase
Gustav Preller
Lawrence Gray

WINNERS OF SUPPLEMENTARY (PUBLICATION) PRIZES

Victor Edward Apps · Rupert Kwan Yun Chan ·
Sally Dellow · Patricia Glinton-Meicholas ·
Lawrence Gray · Patricia W. Grey ·
Andrew Simpson Guthrie · Emily Ho · Henrik Hoeg ·
L.W. (Lawrence) Illsley · Jupy James ·
Akin Jeje (Akinsola Olufemi Jeje) ·
Lelawattee Manoo-Rahming · James Norcliffe ·
Jan Pearson · Jason S Polley · Shahilla Shariff ·
Laura Solomon · James Tam · Dennis Wong

123

THE INTERNATIONAL PROVERSE POETRY PRIZE (SINGLE POEMS)

An annual international Proverse Poetry Prize (for single poems) was established in 2016. The international Proverse Poetry Prize is open to all who are at least eighteen years old whatever their residence, nationality or citizenship.

Single poems, submitted in English, are invited on (a) any subject or theme, chosen by the writer OR (b) on a subject or theme selected by the organizers each year.

Poems may be in any form, style or genre. Each poem should be no more than 30 lines.

Entries should previously be unpublished in any way (except in the case of unpublished translations into English of the entrant's own work already published in another language, providing the entrant holds the copyright).

In 2016, cash prizes were offered as follows:
1st prize; USD100.00; 2nd prize: USD45.00;
3rd prizes (up to four winners): USD20.00.

KEY DATES FOR THE PROVERSE POETRY PRIZE IN 2017 ONWARDS

(subject to confirmation and/or change)

Receipt of entered work, entry forms and entry fees	7 May to 14 July of the year of entry
Announcement of Winners	Before April of the year following the year of entry
Cash Awards Made	At the same time as publication of the winning poems (whether in the Proverse newsletter or website, or in an anthology)
Publication of an anthology of winning and other selected entries	Contingent on the quality of entries in any year

The above information is for guidance only. More information, updated from time to time, is available on the Proverse website: proversepublishing.com

124

POETRY AND POETRY COLLECTIONS
Published by Proverse Hong Kong

Astra and Sebastian, by L.W. Illsley. 2011.
Chasing light, by Patricia Glinton Meicholas. 2013.
China suite and other poems, by Gillian Bickley. 2009.
For the record and other poems of Hong Kong,
by Gillian Bickley. 2003.
Frida Kahlo's Cry and Other Poems,
by Laura Solomon. 2015.
Home, away, elsewhere, by Vaughan Rapatahana. 2011.
Immortelle and bhundaaraa poems,
by Lelawattee Manoo-Rahming. 2011.
In vitro, by Laura Solomon. 2nd ed. 2014.
Irreverent Poems for Pretentious People,
by Henrik Hoeg. 2016.
Moving house and other poems from Hong Kong,
by Gillian Bickley. 2005.
Of Leaves & Ashes, by Patty Ho. 2016.
Of symbols misused, by Mary-Jane Newton. 2011.
Painting the borrowed house: poems,
by Kate Rogers. 2008.
Perceptions, by Gillian Bickley. 2012.
Rain on the pacific coast, by Elbert Siu Ping Lee. 2013.
refrain, by Jason S. Polley. 2010.
Shadow play, by James Norcliffe. 2012.
Shadows in Deferment, by Birgit Bunzel Linder. 2013.
Shifting Sands, by Deepa Vanjani. 2016.
Sightings: a collection of poetry, with an essay, 'communicating poems', by Gillian Bickley. 2007.
Smoked pearl: poems of Hong Kong and beyond,
by Akin Jeje (Akinsola Olufemi Jeje). 2010.
The Burning Lake, by Jonathan Locke Hart. 2016.
The Layers Between (Essays and Poems),
by Celia Claase. 2015.
Unlocking, by Mary-Jane Newton. March 2014.
Wonder, lust & itchy feet, by Sally Dellow. 2011.

125

FIND OUT MORE ABOUT OUR AUTHORS BOOKS, EVENTS AND LITERARY PRIZES

Visit our website:
http://www.proversepublishing.com

Visit our distributor's website: <www.chineseupress.com>

Follow us on Twitter
Follow news and conversation: twitter.com/Proversebooks>
OR
Copy and paste the following to your browser window and follow the instructions:
https://twitter.com/#!/ProverseBooks

"Like" us on www.facebook.com/ProversePress
Request our free E-Newsletter
Send your request to info@proversepublishing.com.

Availability
Most titles are available in Hong Kong and world-wide from our Hong Kong based Distributor,
The Chinese University of Hong Kong Press,
The Chinese University of Hong Kong, Shatin, NT,
Hong Kong SAR, China.
Email: cup-bus@cuhk.edu.hk
Website: <www.chineseupress.com>.
All titles are available from Proverse Hong Kong
http://www.proversepublishing.com
and the Proverse Hong Kong UK-based Distributor.

We have **stock-holding retailers** in Hong Kong,
Singapore (Select Books),
Canada (Elizabeth Campbell Books),
Andorra (Llibreria La Puça, La Llibreria).
Orders can be made from bookshops
in the UK and elsewhere.
Ebooks
Most of our titles are available also as Ebooks.

126

www.ingramcontent.com/pod-product-compliance
Lightning Source LLC
LaVergne TN
LVHW010625100826
845148LV00014B/3109
9789888228553